Tragic Fires Throughout History ™

The *General Slocum* Steamboat Fire of 1904

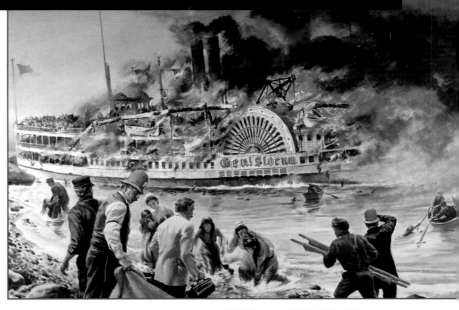

Ellen V. LiBretto

The Rosen Publishing Group, Inc., New York

Published in 2004 by The Rosen Publishing Group, Inc.
29 East 21st Street, New York, NY 10010

First Edition

Library of Congress Cataloging-in-Publication

LiBretto, Ellen V.
  The *General Slocum* steamboat fire of 1904 / by Ellen V. LiBretto. — 1st ed.
     p. cm. — (Tragic fires throughout history)
  Summary: Describes the 1904 fire that destroyed the *General Slocum* and killed more than one thousand people, examining the causes, reactions of passengers, crew, and spectators, and aftermath of the disaster. Includes bibliographical references and index.
  ISBN 0-8239-4486-7 (library binding)
  1. General Slocum (Steamboat)—Juvenile literature. 2. Fires—New York (State)—New York—History—20th century—Juvenile literature. 3. Ships—Fires and fire prevention—New York (State)—New York—History—20th century—Juvenile literature. 4. New York (N.Y.)—History—1898–1951—Juvenile literature. [1. General Slocum (Steamboat) 2. Fires—New York (State)—New York—History—20th century. 3. Ships—Fires and fire prevention. 4. New York, (N.Y.)—Fire, 1904.]
  I. Title. II. Series.
  F128.5.L53 2004
  910'.9163'46—dc21
                                                                         2003010025

Manufactured in the United States of America

CONTENTS

Introduction

The smell of something burning did not worry the happy passengers aboard the steamboat *General Slocum* on the morning of June 15, 1904. Some people thought the smell was coffee burning. Others thought it might be the clam chowder cooking in the galley. More than a thousand people had come out for this boat trip up the East River to the Locust Grove picnic grounds on the Long Island Sound. It was a treat for the congregation of St. Mark's Evangelical Lutheran Church on New York City's Lower East Side to spend a day on the river. For seventeen years, parents and children had looked forward to this annual mid-June boat trip, organized by their minister, Reverend Haas.

Their New York City neighborhood was hot and crowded. Many of the 12,000 residents of Little Germany spoke German and English. They ate German food such as potato salad and sausages and enjoyed other aspects of their German heritage.

Thirteen-year-old Lucy Rosenagel was one of 400 children who took the day off from school for the boat trip. The shopkeepers in the neighborhood, like the bakers and the butchers, had given free tickets to children for the trip. Some

The *General Slocum* docked at New York's Rockaway Beach in 1899. Built in 1891, the steamboat was a favorite among New York–area church groups for their community outings.

children, like eleven-year-old Catherine Gallagher, had never been on a boat before.

Lucy, her sister, Grace, and their mother woke up early that morning to pack a picnic lunch, including the penny pickles for which the German neighborhood was famous. Excited, Lucy put on her white dress, which her mother had washed and starched for the special day. The family walked from their house on Sixth

This editorial cartoon captures the crowded conditions of immigrant neighborhoods in New York City around 1900. Set in the Lower East Side, it depicts a wealthy man scornfully making his way through a street crowded with children. Other New Yorkers recognized that the immigrant community was an essential part of the city's culture.

Street to the Third Street Recreation Pier to board the boat, the wooden steamer known as the *General Slocum*.

The children ran up the wooden gangplank past one of the boat's two giant paddle wheels to the main deck. They raced up the stairs to the promenade deck, already crowded, because this was where the band would be playing. Leaning over the rails of the promenade deck, they looked out at New York Harbor.

Captain William Van Schaick, an old man in a blue uniform, welcomed the passengers to the thirteen-year-old *General Slocum*, one of the largest wooden excursion steamers in New York City. Named after the decorated Civil War general Henry Warner Slocum, the boat could hold up to 2,500 people. The captain was proud of the newly painted white boat with its slick, varnished decks. There were life preservers stowed in the ceiling to keep passengers afloat if the boat sank, and there were hoses and pumps in case of fire. But all these were simple precautions in case of disaster. It was a special day for many, and no one expected what would happen aboard the *General Slocum* that morning.

Once all the passengers boarded, the captain started his steamer up the East River. A band played traditional German songs while the passengers hung over the rails, eating ice cream, sipping clam chowder, enjoying the warm breeze, and waving to people on shore. A dockworker, John Ronan, remarked to a friend how he envied those aboard the boat, those lucky few able to enjoy a workday with a nice boat trip.

Journal for the Seventeenth Annual Excursion

– OF –

St. Marks Evan. Lutheran Church
323-327 6th Street, New York

Wednesday, June 15th, 1904

Dated June 15, 1904, this program outlined the day's activities for the congregation of the St. Mark's Evangelical Lutheran Church.

What these happy passengers did not know was that by the time Ronan made those comments, a small fire was burning in the cargo cabin near the bow of the boat. A crew member had probably carelessly tossed a match there after lighting a lantern or a cigarette. In this cabin were stored old kegs of paint, wooden barrels filled with glasses packed in hay, and spilled oil from a lamp—all ingredients to jump-start a fire. Within minutes, the flames leapt upward to the main deck. The passengers leaning against the rails were in the fire's path. Three girls—screaming and in flames—jumped overboard. One of them hit her head on the paddle wheel as she fell, leaving a trail of blood. Her mother leaned over the rail, calling hysterically to her floating daughter, "Frieda, mien [my] Frieda!" Hearing the mother's piercing wail, the other passengers began to panic. Frieda's mother then threw herself overboard to be with her dying daughter.

Like hundreds of others on the boat, Lucy Rosenagel became separated from her mother and sister. When she turned to grab the life preservers, her mother and sister were gone. At first she tried to tie on a life preserver, but the strings broke. Then the life preserver started to fall apart, leaving a pile of powdered cork on the deck. Lucy grabbed a camp stool and jumped into the water with hundreds of other helpless passengers.

The person who bought this ticket was too sick to attend the St. Mark's Evangelical Church's ill-fated boat excursion.

In just twenty minutes, the great fire would claim the lives of more than 1,000 passengers. President Theodore Roosevelt ordered an immediate federal investigation to determine the cause of the disaster. When all the dead were counted, 600 families had lost a loved one. Other families were completely wiped out. Lucy's neighborhood on the Lower East Side seemed to have vanished.

This book is about the fire aboard the wooden excursion steamer *General Slocum*. The fire aboard the steamboat was the greatest disaster in New York City history until the World Trade Center attack on September 11, 2001.

The Beginning

The steamboat left the Third Street Pier at 9:40 AM and began its journey up the East River past Blackwell's Island (now Roosevelt Island). The first challenge for the captain and his copilots was to navigate the vessel through the hazardous strait called Hell Gate.

The captain and crew watched for submerged rocks and boulders and peered out at the water trying to read the current as the boat steamed toward Ward's Island. According to the "Scrapbook of Newspaper Clippings Relating to the *General Slocum* Steamboat Disaster" at the New-York Historical Society, while the vessel was completing its difficult passage through the strait, twelve-year-old Frank Perditski ran excitedly to the pilot house to warn the captain. "Hey mister, the ship's on fire!" Perditski shouted to the captain. The captain brushed him off and replied, "Shut up, kid, mind your own business."

Meanwhile, on the main deck another small boy approached police officer Albert Van Tassel who was stationed on the boat. He told the officer that the boat was on fire. The officer noticed a plume of smoke. Officer Van Tassel immediately began to help the passengers. The time was 9:55 AM.

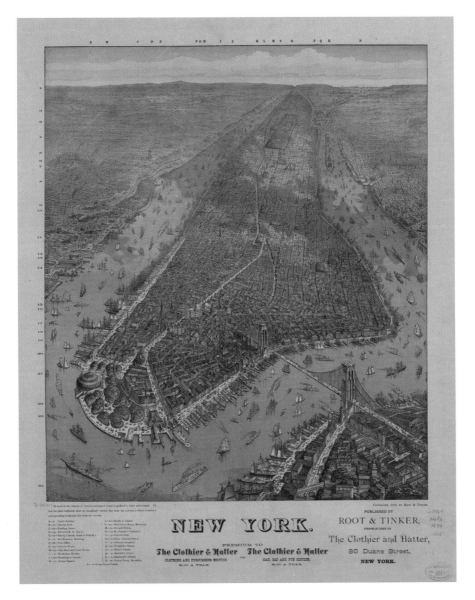

This is an illustration of New York City in 1879. It demonstrates the busy waterways surrounding the island of Manhattan. The boroughs of Brooklyn *(lower right)* and Queens *(upper right)* are also pictured.

Smoke!

John Engelman, a young father, saw dense smoke coming up out of the cargo cabin near the bow of the boat. The *General Slocum* was now at the opening to Hell Gate. Realizing the danger of a fire on a wooden boat, Engelman jumped into the water with his wife and their six-year-old son. The parents made it to shore, but their son was lost in the river.

This photo, taken in 1893, shows how crowded it could be aboard the *General Slocum*. These crowded conditions would fuel the chaos and panic aboard the *Slocum* on June 15, 1904.

Smoke billowed from the port side of the boat. This side was visible to other boats and people on the islands that the boat was passing. From Ward's Island, where the city's mentally ill were hospitalized, patients frantically waved to the passengers. They were trying to let the passengers know that their boat was on fire because they could see the smoke. The passengers ignored them, thinking they were just mentally ill. The passengers who did smell the smoke assumed it was from the food being prepared belowdecks.

The First Warnings

From the other side of the steamer, observers from the mainland community of Astoria, Queens, did not see the smoke. They envied the happy passengers spending a working day aboard the *General Slocum*. According to the "Scrapbook," this is when John Ronan, the dockworker on the Astoria shore, remarked to a friend, "Look at the *Slocum*! Don't it make you hate to work when you see a crowd having as good a time as that." The time was 9:57 AM.

Eight minutes later, a dredge captain on the river sighted the smoke on the lower deck of the *Slocum*. He sounded a shrill alarm to alert Captain Van Schaick that his boat was on fire. It looked like Captain Van Schaick was having trouble getting his signals to his engine room because the boat kept going upriver in spite of the fire.

By 10:05 the *General Slocum* was engulfed in flames.

The Captain and the Fire

How had the fire started? Perhaps a small fire had begun to burn in one of the wooden barrels filled with glasses packed in hay. A boy noticed the fire and alerted a deckhand named Coakley, who slid a door open to investigate. This was the worst thing Coakley could have done. Fire will stay contained behind a closed door. Once Coakley opened the door, he let in oxygen, which fed the flames. Then Coakley made another mistake. He thought he could put out the fire by throwing charcoal on it. The charcoal did not smother the flames.

Today, boats are equipped with sprinkler systems that are activated by the heat of a fire. In those days, these sprinkler systems did not exist. Without a sprinkler system to stop the flames, the small fire aboard the *General Slocum* quickly spread throughout the wooden craft.

Coakley then ran to his boss, First Mate Flanagan. It was Flanagan's job as deck officer to take charge of the emergency. But Flanagan didn't do anything to put out the fire. Instead, he yelled to Captain Van Schaick through the speaking tube: "The ship's on fire!" The fire was now racing up to the deck where passengers were standing.

At a loss as to how to proceed, Flanagan did nothing until he was instructed by the engineer to get the fire hose. He and the other inexperienced deckhands quickly pulled down the hose. The old hose was twisted and kinked and still in a coil on the deck when the water was turned on. The linen hose—the cheapest the Knickerbocker Steamboat Company could buy—could not stand up to the pressure of the water. It burst and broke. The fire hose was useless.

Then the crew attempted to attach a garden hose to the water supply, but the coupling was the wrong size. They gave up before trying out the other pumps and hoses on board that could have aided them in stopping the spread of the fire.

The Captain's Decision

The captain saw the fire charging through the boat like a locomotive. Never having

Although Captain William H. Van Schaick survived the fire, his long career came to an end with the *General Slocum* tragedy.

This diagram of the *General Slocum* shows where the decks collapsed and where the charred remains of several passengers were found.

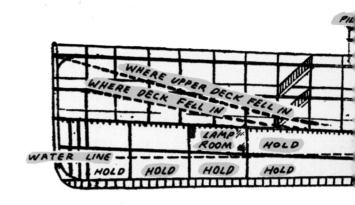

experienced a fire aboard ship, and having had no fire drills with his crew, the captain frantically searched for a landing for his burning craft. The boat increased its speed, passing Ward's Island, and then the swamplands of the Sunken Meadow. The headwinds accelerated the fire forcing many people to jump off in an attempt to escape the raging flames.

Captain Van Schaick bypassed the Bronx shore as a landing site. He was afraid that the burning vessel would ignite the oil tanks, coal yards, lumberyards, ferry slips, and houses located near the shore. Meanwhile, passing craft were sounding warning bells, and other harbor craft were racing toward the *General Slocum* in an attempt to aid the burning boat's passengers and crew.

From the shore at the foot of East 138th Street in the Bronx, a passerby sighted the boat in flames heading toward North Brother

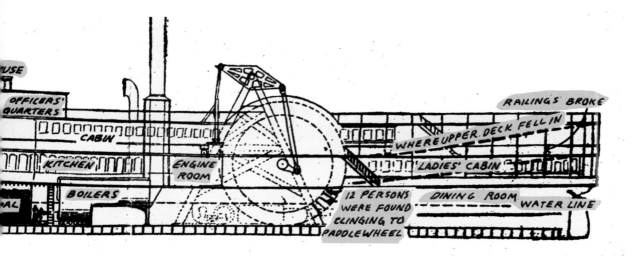

Within the diagram, the following labels appear: OFFICERS' QUARTERS, CABIN, KITCHEN, ENGINE ROOM, BOILERS, 12 PERSONS WERE FOUND CLINGING TO PADDLE WHEEL, DINING ROOM, LADIES' CABIN, WHERE UPPER DECK FELL IN, RAILINGS BROKE, WATER LINE.

Island. According to the "Scrapbook," he telephoned the police, telling them to "bring in all the help they could muster and fast because hundreds of women and children are jumping into the water from the decks."

Captain Van Schaick, who had spent almost fifty years on the water ferrying 30 million passengers over the years, finally made the decision to head for the shore of North Brother Island. It was three miles (4.8 kilometers) away. According to the *New York Times*, he gave the order to First Pilot Edward Van Wart: "Captain Ed, it's all over with her: we can't save her. Keep her jacked up and beach her on North Brother, right ahead, so the people can jump into the shallow water." Fully focused on the landing site, in the pilot house with the windows closed to avoid the flames, Captain Van Schaick gave no direction to the crew to control the fire or to aid the passengers.

Chaos!

The passengers were trapped. Flames rose from the stairway just beyond the forward hold, tearing through the three decks where the passengers were now beginning to react to the disaster. First, a mass of frightened people stampeded to the starboard side of the boat, desperate to flee the flames. But the flames moved faster than the passengers could. The blaze whipped across the decks, igniting hair and clothing. Mothers on fire clutched their babies to their chests and jumped into the water, dropping like stones.

The boat was huge, but there was no place to hide from the flames. They created a red and orange arc from the bow to the stern as the boat sped towards North Brother Island. Many passengers ended up in the river either because they were pushed overboard or they jumped to avoid the flames. Those still on board lunged for the life preservers.

Charles Schwartz, then eighteen years old, was on the bow of the steamer with his friends when the fire was discovered. He formed a bucket brigade to help put out the fire but saw it was hopeless because the fire was moving so fast. Now they knew they had to jump. Schwartz remembered in the "Scrapbook" that the passengers "rushed up to the deck and put on life preservers. Then the rail broke and all of us were thrown into the water. The powdered cork from the life preservers was so thick on the surface of the water that some of us were nearly choked by the stuff."

Eyewitnesses reported that the fire acted like a wall that cut the boat in two. Lucy Rosenagel was one of the many passengers who became separated from her family as the passengers panicked. She

This eyewitness illustration shows a man rushing for a useless life preserver as others are consumed by flames. By the time most people belowdecks realized the ship was on fire, it was too late for them to escape.

This burnt life preserver was retrieved from the scene of the disaster.

had to climb up on a camp stool in order to reach life preservers for her mother, her sister, and herself. When she turned around, they were gone. The life preservers were rotten. While fastening the life preserver around her waist, Lucy watched the strings come off and powdered cork fall out onto the deck. With no options left, Lucy jumped. She showed great resourcefulness by holding on to a camp stool to stay afloat until a passing steamer picked her up. The lifeboats were of no more use to the passengers than the life preservers. None of the crew attempted to take down the lifeboats. They were fastened with wire and stuck to the davits with many layers of old paint, making them impossible to move.

Water: Safe from the Flames

Lucy survived. She recalled later in the "Scrapbook," "So far as I could see, not one of the crew did anything to help the passengers."

Other passengers remembered that most of the crew jumped overboard the minute they heard the fire alarm. Some children jumped as well. Twelve-year-old Louise Gayling, a baby's nurse, held on to the baby with one hand and clutched a floating board with the other. When they were rescued by a passing boat, she could hardly believe that the baby was still alive. Sadly, the baby was the only survivor of the Erckling family, which lost ten members that day.

Another jumper, a crew member called McGrann, was not so lucky. He loaded his pockets with $1,000 in silver coins from the boat's safe, put a life preserver over his head, and jumped overboard. But no life preserver, even in excellent condition, could have saved him. The silver weighed him down, and he was never seen again.

Like Lucy, Reverend Haas lost track of his wife and daughter while reaching for life preservers. He was thrown into the paddle wheel, where he clung to life until he was rescued by a passing tugboat. He never saw his wife and daughter again.

The *Brooklyn Eagle* told the story of young Ellen Breden who forced her way to the rail of the hurricane deck. Her companions begged her not to jump, telling her the river meant sudden death. She jumped anyway, shouting as she jumped, "[I'd] rather die that way than to be burned to death on the boat." She survived; one of her companions did not.

Eleven-year-old Willie Keppler had gone on the excursion without his parents' permission. He was a strong swimmer and loved the water. When the fire overwhelmed the boat, he jumped.

This painting by Sir William Russell Flint illustrates the many boats that rushed to help the passengers of the burning *General Slocum*.

Floating on the river, he witnessed many people jumping, falling, or being pushed from the boat. The water around the flaming boat was hot and most of the passengers could not swim. They clutched at Willie, begging for him to save them. "I tried," Willie remembered later in the *New York Times*, "but they were too big. I had to break away to save myself." Willie was rescued by a passing tug.

Delaying his return home because he feared punishment for cutting school, he spent the night in Harlem. The next day he saw his name in a newspaper. It reported him missing. To relieve his poor parents, he raced home. Expecting to be punished, he got a kiss from his mother and a half-dollar from his father.

A Desperate Rescue

Fireboats, tugs, rowboats, dredges, yachts—about a hundred boats in all—now filled the harbor, attempting to get as close to the burning craft as they could. Very quickly, the scene in the water got ugly. As the passengers fought the strong current, looters in rowboats started grabbing at their jewelry and demanding money in exchange for rescue. August Lutjens, a teenage survivor, told of looters he heard asking two dollars for each desperate drowning passenger they saved.

As the *General Slocum* was rounding Lighthouse Point on the northern tip of North Brother Island, several prisoners from the Rikers Island Prison launched a boat and joined the rescue. They saved five people while they endured the scorching heat and roaring flames. By this time, passengers were even jumping from the upper decks because the flames were reaching straight up from the hold. The boats moved in close so that the passengers could jump right onto them. The heat of the fire was so great that some of the the rescue craft began to burn, too. Everywhere, there were people who helplessly flailed about in the water because they could not swim. Burning debris littered the hot water, and a layer of cork particles released from the rotting life preservers formed over the surface of the water.

Chapter 4

The Run for North Brother Island

"Steamer afire!" shouted John Owens as he looked up from his work on North Brother Island. Two-thirds of the *General Slocum*—looking like a flaming torch—was approaching the landing. Because of its isolated location, North Brother was where New York City kept its contagious disease hospital. Here, patients with diseases like scarlet fever and measles stayed until they got better. John Owens worked there as a mason, or a bricklayer.

Owens made a run for the shore and on the way told the engineer to sound the fire alarm. Grabbing a small boat, Owens immediately set out to rescue passengers. Doctors, nurses, ward helpers, engineers, health inspectors, laborers, and even patients followed close behind him to help. They set up first-aid stations on the grass.

The Beaching

Fewer than fifteen minutes after the fire started, the huge excursion boat came to a final halt. It was 10:10 AM. Beached with its burning bow in about 7 feet (2 meters) of water, the *General Slocum* was stuck at an angle that would make rescue nearly impossible. The stern was in water way over people's heads, about 50 feet (15 m) from the shore.

There were now 400 to 600 people taking refuge at the stern on the starboard side of the hurricane deck. The enormous strain of the weight of the crowd and the flames that filled the air was tipping the boat into the water. Thomas Miley, from a rowboat about 100 feet (30.5 m) away from the *General Slocum*, witnessed the moment when the hurricane deck exploded into flames. The "Scrapbook" captured what Miley saw: "Cries of horror went up from every deck and in an instant, it seemed the rails were swept away as if they were made of paper." The passengers were thrown into the water, most drowning instantly.

Captain Van Schaick and his copilots opened the window of the pilot house, jumped out, and swam to shore. Arriving wounded on North Brother Island, the three men were questioned and then arrested by police. The captain's first pilot, Edward Van Wart, was later criticized for the careless way he beached the vessel. If only he had beached the boat in shallow water, the passengers could have waded to shore.

The Rescue at North Brother Island

The men from the hospital staff were the first in the water to rescue some of the passengers. Meanwhile, women dragged

This photograph shows rescuers searching for survivors and victims of the *General Slocum* fire in the waters off North Brother Island. A ladder used in the operation can also be seen in the photograph. Mary McCann *(inset)* was widely hailed for her courageous participation in the rescue.

35-foot (11-m) ladders to the water's edge to serve as lifelines. When they pulled the ladders from the river, half-drowned bodies clung to the rungs. Standing in water up to their necks, other rescuers formed human chains to pass the badly burned victims to safety. About 150 people were rescued.

Doctors raced against time to save the unconscious passengers who had been pulled from the water. Nurses tended to the burns of the victims. Sixteen-year-old Mary McCann, recovering from measles, was an excellent swimmer. She ran into the water and swam out many times, rescuing nine children. Five years later, she was recognized for her heroism by being awarded a Gold Lifesaving Medal in Washington, D.C.

Captain John Wade saw the fire raging off North Brother Island from his tugboat, the *Wade*. He positioned his tug alongside the burning vessel so that he was able to catch women and children thrown to safety from the boat by Officer Van Tassel.

Officer Van Tassel was still tossing passengers into passing boats when the hurricane deck collapsed. In the "Scrapbook," Van Tassel describes what happened next: "Suddenly a sheet of flame and smoke came through the main deck. The flames were on the port side and everyone rushed starboard." Then all the women panicked, and Van Tassel said they "fell like rain into the water."

As passengers were dropping from the upper deck of the *General Slocum* and onto the deck of the tug, Captain Wade ignored the heat and flames. His crew jumped into the water pulling bodies onto the *Wade*. When the tug was full, he raced to shore to drop off the survivors. With his tug in flames, he returned to the burning vessel and continued to rescue the helpless people. "Let her burn," he said, according to *Munsey's Magazine*. "What's a tug to human life?" Captain Wade and his crew rescued 155 people, and he received a Medal of Honor from his congressman.

Officer Van Tassel was eventually thrown into the water by the collapse of the hurricane deck. He found himself going under the water as the helpless passengers reached out to him. Overwhelmed with cries for assistance from the many passengers who could not swim, he discovered that by turning on his back, he became a human float. He reached the shore of North Brother Island with many survivors clinging to him.

When it became nearly impossible to imagine that there could be any life left aboard the boat that now burned like an inferno, a small boy, about six years old, desperate to escape the flames on the deck, was climbing the flagstaff. The rescuers watched

This photo captures the grisly scene as the bodies of the *General Slocum* fire victims are laid out on North Brother Island.

helplessly as he inched his way up the pole. When he was almost at the top, with a boat at the ready to catch him, the pole collapsed and the little blond boy was lost forever.

The End

By 10:20 AM, it was all over. The great fire took less than thirty minutes to steal the lives of 1,021 passengers and 5 crew members. The brave rescuers on North Brother Island had only ten minutes before the once-proud steamboat *General Slocum* became a charred wreck. By the afternoon, the green grass on North Brother Island was covered with corpses. The scene looked like the aftermath of a battle.

The charred remains of the *General Slocum* sink to their final resting place off the shore of North Brother Island.

Some survivors were fortunate to find some of their family members alive. Six-month-old Adella Liebenow Wotherspoon and her mother were reunited with her father. Both parents suffered severe burns, and Adella lost two sisters, two cousins, and an aunt.

Aftermath

It was the coroner's grisly task to identify the bodies of the recovered dead. All money and jewelry were removed and tagged. The time on all watches of the recovered dead was between 10:20 and 10:25 AM. Hundreds of burned corpses were placed like dominoes on the grass of North Brother Island.

Corpses were put on ice for later identification by family members. Nearly every emergency vehicle in New York was used to take the wounded to hospitals and the dead to the morgue. Thirty thousand people would come to the morgue with the hopes of identifying their friends and relatives.

Lucy Rosenagel visited the coroner to see if she could recover any of her mother's jewelry. She told him how she saved herself by using a campstool as a raft. She described how she had seen others hanging on to the rail of the boat. One woman had dropped into the water after a man bit her hand to take her place on the rail.

Amid the almost unbearable grief under the heavy weight of so many deaths, a miracle happened. Two babies had washed ashore and they were alive! Picked up by a boat near the sinking steamer, they were taken to Lebanon Hospital. As hundreds of people filed past the unidentified babies, a cry of pure joy was heard. A grandmother carrying a picture of her grandson ran to embrace one of the babies. His name was Charles Debbert. He was taken on the excursion with his mother, who did not survive.

This submarine diver recovered many of the victims' bodies from the sunken wreck of the *General Slocum*.

For weeks, the ebb and flow of the tides carried the bodies to the New York City shore, as divers continued the search. S. H. Berg, one of the divers to bring up the rail from the upper deck, discovered four women burned with their hands entwined with rope as they clung to the rail before the collapse. Divers pulled up many people who were carrying large sums of money, bankbooks, and stock certificates sewn into their clothes. Looters in rowboats crept out at night to strip the dead of their valuables.

A stream of hearses eighty blocks long brought the dead to their graves. A hundred thousand mourners lined the streets of Little Germany to say good-bye to their friends and relatives. The sixty-one unidentified dead were buried in the Lutheran cemetery across the water in Queens. A monument to the thousand plus victims marks the gravesite.

Horse-drawn hearses carry the bodies of a Brooklyn family—all the members of which died in the *General Slocum* fire—to the Lutheran cemetery in Middle Village, Queens.

Devastation in Little Germany

In Little Germany, nearly every family was touched by the tragedy. Flags around the neighborhood hung at half-mast. When school reopened, the rows of empty seats told the story of the catastrophe. Graduation exercises were called off. School officials recommended that all children learn to swim. Other Sunday schools that had planned boat trips cancelled them. Few children now played and laughed on the sidewalks as half of all those who died were under the age of twenty. In Tompkins Square Park, where many of the 400 young victims had played, the Slocum Memorial Fountain reminds us today of the tragedy that took place a century ago.

The neighborhood would never be the same again. To escape the sadness, many German Americans moved uptown to Yorkville or across the river to Queens and Brooklyn, and some even returned to Germany. Many Germans were replaced by new immigrants who spoke Italian and Yiddish.

The Government Report

President Theodore Roosevelt immediately ordered a federal investigation into the causes of the accident. A commission determined that a sequence of errors caused by faulty equipment, carelessness, poor judgment, and disregard for steamboat safety regulations all contributed to the tragedy. They interviewed many survivors, the crew, the vessel's owners (the Knickerbocker Steamboat Company), and the owners of the company that provided the life preservers. Although the commission never determined the exact cause of the fire, it concluded that the fire began in the storeroom in the hold, where flammable materials were stored.

Flammable materials like paint, machine oil, and kerosene, along with the hay used to protect the beer glasses from breakage, were probably ignited by a carelessly tossed match. The wooden boat was a tinderbox, and the passengers never had a chance of surviving a fire. In addition, the report noted, the crew, most of

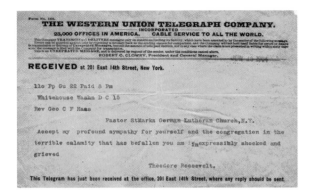

President Theodore Roosevelt sent this telegram to the congregation of the St. Mark's Evangelical Lutheran Church soon after he got news of the terrible fire.

whom jumped ship, acted in a cowardly manner. They did nothing to put out the fire or to save the passengers.

Five government inspectors were dismissed for their faulty inspection methods involving the *General Slocum*. The company that manufactured the rotten life preservers, which were also later found to contain several ounces of iron, was fined.

The Captain's Fate

It was determined at the inquest that Captain Van Schaick used poor judgment by not beaching his craft sooner. Eyewitnesses reported that the fire started as early as Ninety-second Street off Blackwell's Island at the entrance to Hell Gate. The captain's testimony about where the boat was when he was informed about the fire contradicted itself. His decision to make the run to North Brother Island has been debated by historians for decades. Was beaching the boat at North Brother Island a good decision? Could he have beached it sooner? The government commission, however, stated that the captain knew about the fire before the steamer passed the eastern end of Ward's Island. The commission believed that the captain could have then beached the vessel on Sunken Meadow or in the Bronx Kill, perhaps saving hundreds of lives in the process.

Two years after the disaster, Captain Van Schaick was tried and convicted. The jury found him guilty of failing to train his crew at fire drills and of keeping his fire equipment in poor shape. At his trial, the captain, blinded in one eye by the fire, squinted at the jury, shocked at the verdict of ten years' imprisonment. Even some of the

Frank Barnaby (*right*), president of the Knickerbocker Steamboat Company, is seen testifying at the investigation of the *General Slocum* fire disaster.

THE REPORT AT A GLANCE

The government commission recommended the following to insure better safety on wooden steamboats:

- Fireproof bulkheads, hatches, and so on.

- Life preservers in good working condition for all passengers

- Fire hose of the best quality, with standard coupling devices

- Hand fire extinguishers located throughout the vessel

- Installation of sprinkler system in cargo and freight areas

- Life boat installation for easy removal

survivors felt it was an unusually harsh sentence for an old man who claimed that he had done his best to save the passengers.

Captain Van Schaick said that he had been a victim of an act of God. "What is there for me to say?" he asked, according to the *New York Times*. "I am an old man now. I have followed the sea for more than fifty years . . . this is a pretty tough finish, but my counsel tells me I surely will have another chance and I hope I will." Captain Van Schaick served three years of his ten-year sentence before it was changed by President William Howard Taft. He lived with his wife on his farm for many years. He died at age ninety.

Remembering the Tragedy

Through determination, bravery, and luck, a fortunate few survived what was to become the greatest peacetime maritime disaster in United States history. Many of those survivors escaped with serious injuries. In all, 600 families suffered a loss while many families were completely wiped out.

In the old neighborhood that was once called Little Germany, there is a fountain in Tompkins Square Park that reminds us of the tragedy. Written on the fountain are the words, "They were the Earth's purest children, young and fair." Each year on June 15, a wreath is placed on the fountain in memory of the lives of the children who once played there.

Last Survivor Still Remembers

In 1906, Adella Liebenow Wotherspoon was two years old when she pulled the cord that unveiled the statue over the great grave in the Lutheran cemetery where the sixty-one unidentified are buried. A retired school teacher, Wotherspoon is the last survivor of the

Adella Wotherspoon, ninety-nine when this photo was taken *(top)*, is the last living survivor of the *General Slocum* tragedy. At age two *(bottom left)*, Wotherspoon attended the unveiling of the monument to the sixty-one unidentified victims buried at the Lutheran cemetery in Queens. This newspaper clipping *(bottom right)* appeared in the *World* in 1906.

General Slocum fire. While she was just a baby at the time of the fire, Wotherspoon's mother told her about the family's experience on the burning boat. Her mother, with her hair on fire, covered her baby's face. With her own clothing on fire, she fell into the water during the panic. Luckily both she and her baby were scooped up by a boat, the *Franklin Edson*, and taken to North Brother Island. Wotherspoon's father and uncle stayed on the burning boat, looking for other family members until their clothes caught fire. They then jumped into the water. They survived as well.

The loss of her two sisters, cousins, and aunt stayed with Adella Wotherspoon always. After the tragedy, her mother was frightened of the water and dreaded taking the ferry to the annual *Slocum* memorial services.

Wotherspoon has kept the story of the disaster alive with frayed and yellowed scrapbooks, assembled by her father as therapy to work his way through his grief. (Wotherspoon's father died in 1911 from burns he suffered in the fire.) In the scrapbooks there is an article from the *World*, dated June 16, 1906, with a photograph of two-year-old Wotherspoon, with the headline, "Youngest Slocum Survivor, a Baby Unveils the Monument."

Commemoration of an almost forgotten tragic event like the disastrous fire aboard the *General Slocum* nearly a hundred years ago serves as a study in the two sides of human nature. It shows us how people may behave in great distress. Some act with courage and sacrifice, others with cowardice and selfishness. There were those who showed selfless dedication in their rescue

This monument was unveiled on the first anniversary of the *General Slocum* tragedy, June 15, 1905. Engraved on the monument is the inscription "Burning of the steamboat *General Slocum* on the East River June 15, 1904 in which 1,020 lives were lost."

efforts, while others demanded a price for saving lives. The tragedy also demonstrates the fact that even very experienced professionals may misjudge a most dangerous situation, with tragic consequences.

Timeline

(Times are approximate, based on time variations on people's watches and on eyewitness testimony.)

9:40 AM
General Slocum steamboat leaves the Third Street Recreation Pier in lower Manhattan heading to Locust Grove on Long Island Sound.

9:53
General Slocum starts through the perilous waters of Hell Gate.

9:55
Frank Perditski, a twelve-year-old passenger, notifies Captain Van Schaick in the pilot house that he sees smoke, as the boat is going through Hell Gate.

9:57
John E. Ronan, a dockworker on the Astoria shore, remarks to a friend about the good time the people on board are having.

9:59
A boy tells deckhand Coakley that smoke is coming up a stairway.

10:04
Coakley alerts First Mate Flanagan.

10:05
William Alloway, a dredge captain, sights smoke on the lower deck of the *Slocum* and sounds an alarm.

10:06
Flanagan tells Captain Van Schaick that the boat is on fire.

10:07
The captain heads to North Brother Island.

10:10
The *General Slocum* is beached at North Brother Island.

10:20
The boat is an inferno.

10:20–10:25
Times stopped on all the watches of the recovered dead.

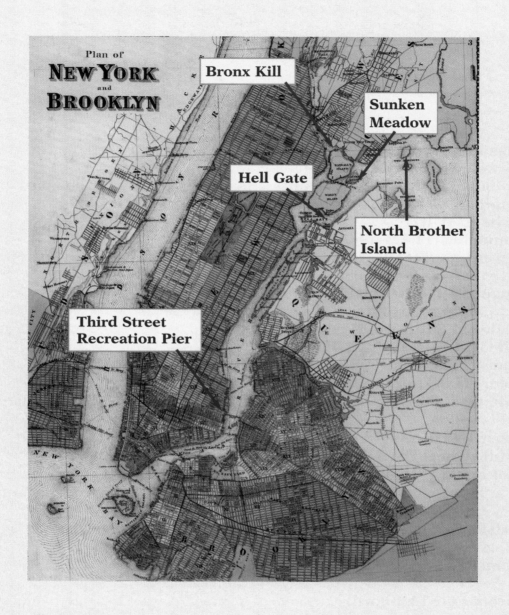

Plan of
NEW YORK
and
BROOKLYN

Bronx Kill

Sunken Meadow

Hell Gate

North Brother Island

Third Street Recreation Pier

This map of New York City, done in 1868, shows the route the *General Slocum* took on that fateful day in 1904.

Glossary

brigade (brih-GAYD) A group of people organized to work together.

buoyancy (BOY-an-see) The ability to float.

combustible (kom-BUST-i-buhl) Capable of catching fire and burning.

coupling (CUP-ling) Device for joining two parts.

davits (DAV-itz) Devices used to raise or lower boats on a ship.

flammable (FLAM-a-buhl) Easily set on fire.

forward hold (FOR-werd HOLD) Area toward the front of a boat in the cargo compartment.

gangplank (GANG-plank) Small movable bridgelike structure for use by persons boarding or leaving a ship at a pier.

headwind (HED-wind) A wind opposed to the course of a moving ship.

hull (HUL) The body or shell of a ship.

inquest (IN-kwest) An examination of a case by a judge or a jury.

looters (LOOT-erz) Robbers.

main deck (MAYN DEK) The uppermost deck, running the full length of a ship.

nozzle (NAH-zel) The spout on a hose.

paddle wheel (PAH-dul WEEL) A wheel for propelling a ship.

pilot house (PIH-lot HOWZ) A compartment on or near the bridge of a ship that contains the steering wheel and means of communicating with the engine room.

portside (PORT-syd) The side of the ship that is on the left side of a person facing forward.

promenade deck (PRAH-men-odd DEK) The upper deck on a passenger ship where passengers can take walks.

starboard (STAR-bord) The side of a ship that is on the right when a person faces forward.

steamboat (STEEM-boht) A steam-driven vessel used on inland waters.

stern (STERHN) The back of a ship.

For More Information

Web Sites

Due to the changing nature of Internet links, the Rosen Publishing Group, Inc., has developed an online list of Web sites related to the subject of this book. This site is updated regularly. Please use this link to access the list:

http://www.rosenlinks.com/tfth/gsff

For Further Reading

Cussler, Clive, and Craig Dirgo. *The Sea-Hunters II: More True Adventures with Famous Shipwrecks*. New York: G. P. Putnam's Sons, 2002.
Rust, Claud. *The Burning of the General Slocum*. New York: Elsevier/ Nelson, 1981.

Bibliography

"1904 *General Slocum* Disaster." *The Brooklyn Eagle.* Retrieved January
 2003 (http://freepages.genealogy.rootsweb.com/~blkyn/Newspaper/
 Slocum/Slocum.html).
Casson, Herbet N. *Munsey's Magazine.* December 1904. New York: The
 New York Historical Society, microfilm, pp. 324–330.
Cussler, Clive, and Craig Dirgo. *The Sea-Hunters II: More True Adventures
 with Famous Shipwrecks.* New York: G. P. Putnam's Sons, 2002.
New York Historical Society. "Scrapbook of Newspaper Clippings
 Relating to the *General Slocum* Steamboat Disaster," microfilm, 1904.
New York Times. June 19, 1904. New York: The New-York Historical
 Society, microfilm, p. 1.
New York Times. January 28, 1906. New York: The New York Historical
 Society, microfilm, p. 1.
Report of the U.S. Commission of Investigation Upon Disaster to Steamer
 General Slocum. Washington, DC: U.S.G.P.O., microform, 1904.
Rust, Claud. *The Burning of the General Slocum.* New York:
 Elsevier/Nelson, 1981.
Scrapbook of newspaper clippings related to the *General Slocum* fire,
 collected by Paul Liebenow, father of Adella Liebenow Wotherspoon.
"Stories Told by Survivors." *The Brooklyn Eagle.* June 20, 1904.
 Brooklyn, NY.: The New York-Historical Society microfilms.
Wotherspoon, Adella L., interview by author, Watchung, NJ,
 December 9, 2002.

Index

About the Author

Ellen V. LiBretto is a fifth-generation New Yorker who grew up hearing the tragic story of the *General Slocum* disaster from her great aunt Carrie, who lost her best friend in the fire on the boat. She is an author, marketing consultant, and librarian who has held management positions at the New York City Public Libraries and Random House. Her previous books in the area of teen literacy include four editions of *The High/Low Handbook*, published by Libraries Unlimited. She lives in New York City with her husband, Adam Conrad. Besides reading, Ellen and her husband enjoy hiking and traveling.

Acknowledgments

I would like to thank Robert Miller, transportation historian; Frank Duffy, photographer and journalist; Mrs. Adella Wotherspoon, survivor of the *General Slocum* fire; and my husband, Adam Conrad, for their help in providing historical details and support. Their expertise on the history of the *General Slocum* tragedy enabled me to tell the story of this missing piece of New York City history to children who will now know that this event—which took place almost a century before the dreadful day of September, 11, 2001—also changed the lives of thousands of people forever.

Photo Credits

Cover, pp. 1, 8, 16–17, 19, 32 courtesy of the Claude Rust Collection; p. 5 Queens Borough Public Library, Long Island Division, Frederick W. Weber Collection; pp. 6, 26 Culver Pictures; p. 9 Queens Historical Society, Gift of Robert C. Kuenster; p. 11 Library of Congress, Geography and Map Division; p. 12 Society for the Preservation of New England Antiquities; pp. 15, 20, 29, 31, 35 collection of the New-York Historical Society; p. 22 The Illustrated London News Picture Library, London, UK/Bridgeman Art Library; pp. 26 (inset), 38 Maura B. McConnell; p. 28 © AP/Wide World Photos; p. 34 Archives of the Metropolitan New York Synod, Evangelical Lutheran Church in America; p. 40 courtesy of Ellen V. LiBretto; p. 43 © David Rumsey Collection.

Designer: Les Kanturek; Editor: Charles Hofer; Photo Researcher: Amy Feinberg